New Hampshire Fish Species

Game Fish & Panfish

Billy Grinslott & Kinsey Marie Books

ISBN - 9781968228545

Banded Sunfish got their name because they have darker lines that run vertically on their sides. They also have a rounded tail with spots on their body, tail and fins. Banded sunfish are typically only about 2 inches long, making them one of the smallest sunfish. Their small size makes them vulnerable to larger fish, so they thrive in protected areas. Banded sunfish prefer slow-moving, vegetated waters like swamps, ponds, and backwaters of creeks

The Pumpkinseed is also known as pond perch, sun perch, and punky's sunfish. It can be found in numerous lakes, ponds, and rivers. It is their body shape resembling the seed of a pumpkin, that inspired their name. Pumpkinseed sunfish have speckles on their orangish colored sides and back, with a yellow to orange belly and chest. They are active during the day and rest at night near the bottom or in shelter areas.

The bluegill also considered a sunfish is the most popular fish to fish for. They are called pan fish because they are about the size of a frying pan. Bluegills love to eat insects and bugs. They have good vision and rely on their keen eyesight to feed. Three types in this group are the Bluegill, Sunfish, and Pumpkinseed.

The Green Sunfish is blue green in color. It has yellow flecks on both its scales and some parts of its sides. The Green Sunfish also has broken blue stripes which is why some people confuse it with the Bluegill. Green Sunfish are very adaptable. They can live in any body of water that has vegetation or weeds. Green sunfish are opportunistic feeders, consuming insects, small fish, and other invertebrates.

The Redbreast sunfish has a red-yellow chest and belly with rusty brown spots on their body. The species is known for its distinctive grunting vocalizations, which are produced by grinding their teeth together. Redbreast sunfish are capable of surviving in oxygen-poor environments by using their gills to extract oxygen from air bubbles trapped in aquatic vegetation.

The Rock Bass is not actually a bass but a member of the sunfish family. The biggest Rock Bass ever caught on record weighs about three pounds and was a little over one foot long. Rock bass prefer waters with rocky vegetated areas, that's how they got their name.

Sculpins are small, bottom-dwelling fish with a flattened body shape, large pectoral fins, and a unique camouflage pattern, often found in clear, fast-flowing waters with rocky substrates, and they are known for their ambush hunting tactics. Sculpins have very large mouths and can swallow items nearly as large as themselves. They Prefer cold, well-oxygenated, rocky-bottomed lakes and streams, often found at very deep depths.

Blueback herring are small, silver-blue anadromous fish that migrate to freshwater rivers in spring to spawn. They have a deep, bluish green back, silvery sides, a forked tail, and a black abdominal lining. They are typically 8 to 11 inches long but can reach up to 15 inches in length. They prefer swift-flowing, rocky, or gravel-bottomed rivers for spawning, though they can inhabit landlocked, freshwater lakes.

The burbot, also known as the eel pout. They get their name because they have a serpent-like or eel-like body. They can wrap their tail around things. There's nothing to worry about if you catch one, they may try to wrap their tail around your arm, but they are harmless. Burbots are adapted to cold water and are found in large, cold rivers, lakes, and reservoirs, primarily preferring freshwater habitats. Burbots are also known as eelpout, lingcod, and lawyer. The biggest burbot ever caught in New Hampshire weighed 12 pounds, 8.48 ounces.

There are two main types of crappies. The white crappie and the black crappie. They are also members of the sunfish family. The difference between the white and black crappie is one has dark spots and the other has dark lines and is lighter in color. The white crappie has six dorsal fin spines, whereas the black crappie has eight dorsal fin spines. The white crappie can grow bigger and more of the bigger white crappie are caught in North America. The biggest black crappie caught in New Hampshire weighed 2 lbs. 15.84 oz.

The black, brown and yellow bullhead are part of the catfish family. They usually only grow to about 10 inches long. They use their whiskers to help find food. The bullhead is the most common member of the catfish family. Bullheads live in the water containing low oxygen levels. They can survive on low oxygen areas, where other fish can't. The largest brown bullhead ever recorded in New Hampshire weighed 3 pounds 4.8 ounces.

The Margined Madtom is a small, 3–6-inch freshwater catfish, identifiable by the dark brown/black margins on its tail, dorsal, and anal fins. Inhabiting rocky, clear streams and rivers, they are nocturnal, feed on aquatic insects, and possess mildly venomous pectoral spines that cause a painful sting. These fish are nocturnal, hiding under boulders during the day, and feed on insects, and crustaceans.

White catfish are interesting because they are smaller than other common catfish species like channel catfish, they have a wider head and lack the black spots of channel catfish. White catfish are the smallest of the large North American catfish species. The White catfish has white chin barbells, which distinguish it from other species. There are four pairs of barbels, whiskers around the mouth, two on the chin, one at the angle of the mouth, and one behind the nostril.

Channel Catfish are the most fished catfish species with around 8 million anglers fishing for them per year. Channel catfish have taste buds all over their body, making them highly sensitive to the taste and smell of food. They also have barbels (whiskers) around their mouths, which are used for sensing and tasting food. They use sound waves to communicate with each other. They can also produce alarm substances to warn other catfish of danger. The biggest channel catfish ever caught in New Hampshire weighed 15 pounds, 12.8 ounces.

White perch grow seven to ten inches in length and rarely weigh more than one pound. They have a silvery body with faint lines on the sides. The white perch is an opportunistic feeder. Young feed primarily on zooplankton and adults feed on aquatic insect larvae, minnows and fish eggs. White Perch is a euryhaline species, inhabiting fresh, brackish and coastal waters. The largest White Perch ever caught in New Hampshire weighed 3 lbs., 11.5 oz. and measured 17.20 inches

The sucker fish has the same mouth as a carp. They got their name because their mouth is like a suction cup. They normally are bottom feeders and suck their food from the bottom of the lake. Many people use sucker fish to fish for northern pike and other big game fish. The record for the largest White Sucker caught in New Hampshire is a 6-lb. 11.68oz. fish.

Fallfish are the largest native minnow species in eastern North America, often reaching 15-18 inches in length and weighing over 2 pounds, inhabiting clear, rocky streams. They are known for building massive, pyramid-shaped nests from rocks, with males creating structures that can reach 6 feet in diameter and weigh up to 2 tons. They are silvery with dark-edged scales, a dark stripe along the back, and a large, blunt snout.

The two most famous perches are the common perch and the yellow perch. The yellow perch has a brilliant greenish yellow color with orange fins. The yellow perch is the biggest one and can grow to a size of 18 inches. It's also known as the jumbo perch. The other type of perch is the white perch. The largest yellow perch in New Hampshire was 15.5 inches in length.

Carp have long been an important food fish to humans. Carp are bottom feeders for the most part and their mouth is made like a suction cup, so they can suck food off the bottom. Carp are good for a lake because they help clean the bottom of the lake. The largest carp recorded in New Hampshire is a 41-pound, 0.04-ounce (40.5-inch) common carp

Smallmouth bass have a smaller mouth than the largemouth bass. They also have different markings and are lighter in color. They don't live in most lakes because they prefer living in colder water. They are typically found in the northern states in America because the water is cooler. The current world record smallmouth is an 11-pound, 15-ounce fish. The official New Hampshire state record for Smallmouth bass is a 7-pound, 14.5-ounce fish measuring 23.25 inches.

The largemouth bass is the most sought-after bass in North America. Largemouth bass live in just about every lake in North America. They have great hearing and can hear a crayfish crawling on the bottom of the lake. The largest largemouth bass ever caught in New Hampshire weighed 10 pounds, 8 ounces.

The walleye got its name because of its white looking eyes. Their eyes collect light, even in low light conditions. This means they can see in the dark. Because they can see in the dark, they mostly feed at night. During the daytime their eyes are very sensitive, so they usually head for deeper water or shady places. Walleye like to live in cooler water and are normally found in the upper part of North America. The biggest walleye ever caught in New Hampshire weighed 12 lbs. 8.8 oz.

Pickerel kind of look like northern pike, but they are not. The Pike is larger in size than the Pickerel. The Pickerel has more spots than the Pike, but the Pike has spots on its fins and pickerel don't. Pickerel has a dark bar beneath their eyes and northern pike don't. Pickerel are also known as gunfish or slime darts. The record for the largest Chain Pickerel ever caught in New Hampshire is an 8-pound fish measuring 26 inches in length.

The Northern Pike is one of the most sought-after fish for anglers. It got its name because it likes to live in cooler water mainly in the northern states of North America. The northern pike is a very aggressive predator. They don't like to live in groups with other fish, they are very territorial and like to live alone. Their behavior is closely affected by weather conditions. The largest Northern Pike ever caught in New Hampshire weighed 26 pounds 9.44 ounces.

The Redfin Pickerel is a small, solitary freshwater fish in the pike family, typically measuring 10–15 inches and living 8–10 years. They inhabit clear, slow-moving, heavily vegetated streams and swamps. They are ambush predators feeding on small fish, crustaceans, and insects. They are olive to yellowish green with distinct, bright red-orange fins and a dark, backwards-slanting bar beneath the eye.

Another breed of the Muskie is the tiger muskie. The tiger muskie is a cross between the northern pike and muskie. They grow larger and faster than normal muskies and northern pikes. The tiger muskie got its name because it has tiger like stripes. Tiger Muskies are very rare and hard to catch. Known as "the fish of 10,000 casts," they are difficult to catch, requiring heavy tackle, strong lines, and robust leaders to handle their teeth and power. The largest tiger muskellunge recorded in New Hampshire weighed 11 lbs. 11.68 oz. and measured 35.50 inches.

Alewives are anadromous fish that migrate from the ocean to freshwater rivers and streams to spawn. They are small, silvery herring-like fish with a saw-edged belly and a forked tail. Alewives have a distinctive saw-edge on their belly, formed by modified scales called scutes. This feature is used for protection and is also what gives them the nickname saw bellies. While most alewives are anadromous, there are also populations that have become landlocked.

Lake whitefish are related to salmon and trout. They are known for their deep-bodied, silvery appearance and are a major part of the Great Lakes ecosystem. They typically grow to 17-22 inches and range from 1.5-4 pounds. Whitefish are a popular and valuable commercial fish, generating the greatest income for Great Lakes commercial fisheries. Lake whitefish are also known as Lake Superior whitefish, whiting, and shad. The largest Lake whitefish ever caught in New Hampshire weighed 5 pounds, 1 ounce.

Sturgeons have sharp spines on their back, so be careful when handling them. Instead of scales, sturgeon skin is covered in bony plates called scutes, which can be very sharp on young sturgeon. Sturgeons have been around since the dinosaur days. Sturgeons mostly live in large, freshwater lakes and rivers. The largest sturgeon caught in New Hampshire was a 85-pound fish.

Cusk fish, like the Atlantic cusk are bottom-dwelling fish. They have elongated, eel-like bodies with dorsal and anal fins merged into a continuous fin along the tail. They are part of the cod family. They prefer hard, rocky bottoms and can be found in depths of 30 to 1000 meters. They can grow up to 3 to 3.5 feet long. The largest cusk fish caught in New Hampshire is 35 inches long and weighed 12 pounds, 8.48 ounces.

Round Whitefish are interesting freshwater fish known for their cylindrical shape and unique features like a single flap between their nostrils. They have larger scales compared to other salmonids, and their scales on the back are edged with black. They are found in cool, clear waters of lakes and rivers, often in deep areas. While some can grow to over 22 inches, the average size is between 8 and 12 inches.

The rainbow trout gets its name because of its brilliant colors. Rainbow trout populations are good indicators of water pollution because they can only survive in clean waters. They like to live in rivers and streams. Rainbow trout rank among the top five most sought game fish in North America. The largest rainbow trout ever recorded in the state weighed 12 lbs. 9.12 oz.

Brown trout can live up to 20 years. Brown trout have higher tolerance for warmer waters than either brook or rainbow trout. Brown trout can be found on almost every continent except Antarctica, and many can be found living in the ocean. The record for the largest Brown trout ever caught in New Hampshire is 16 lbs. 6 oz.

Brook trout are characterized by their olive-green bodies with pale, worm-like markings, red spots with bluish halos, and orange-red fins with white and black edges. They can grow up to 12 inches in length. Brook trout are cold-water fish that prefer clean, clear, and cold streams, lakes, and ponds. The biggest brook trout ever caught in New Hampshire was a 9-pound, 25.5-inch fish.

Splake Trout are a hybrid resulting from the crossing of a male brook trout and a female lake trout. They are known for their rapid growth, allowing them to reach a catchable size quickly. Splake are often stocked in cold-water lakes and ponds. They are found in deep water during the summer to avoid high water temperatures and feed on open-water prey, like lake trout.

Atlantic salmon are anadromous, meaning they live in both freshwater and saltwater. Many Atlantic Salmon are present in New Hampshire, primarily as landlocked fish in inland lakes and tributaries rather than sea-run fish. They are known for their impressive leaping abilities, allowing them to jump over waterfalls and obstacles to reach spawning grounds. Atlantic salmon change color when they spawn, becoming a rusty-bronze color with red markings. The largest landlocked Atlantic salmon recorded in New Hampshire was 18 pounds 8 ounces, and measuring 34.5 inches.

The lake trout is one of the biggest of the trout family. The biggest lake trout caught was 72 pounds. Lake trout like to live in lakes that are deep. They like being in the cool water in the deep parts of a lake. They have been reported to live up to 70 years in some Canadian lakes. The largest lake trout caught in New Hampshire weighed 37.65 pounds and measured over 40 inches long.

Fun Facts About New Hampshire Fish

1 - The brook trout is the state fish. Brook trout are found in nearly every small, cold stream across the state.

2 - Unlike other trout, the brook trout lack teeth on the roof of their mouth. They rely on their bottom teeth to grab food.

3 - The lake sturgeon is the granddaddy of all fish. They can live up to 100 years and weigh up to 200 pounds.

4 - The largest freshwater fish caught in New Hampshire is a 37.65-pound lake trout measuring over 41 inches.

5 – The banded sunfish is generally considered one of the smallest fish species in New Hampshire, rarely exceeding 3.5 inches

6 - The burbot, also known as eelpout, has an odd habit of wrapping its slimy tail around the hand or arm of anglers.

7 – New Hampshire is home to approximately 80 native species of freshwater fish that inhabit its lakes, rivers, and streams.

Author Page

Billy Grinslott & Kinsey Marie Books

ISBN – 9781968228545

Thanks

www.ingramcontent.com/pod-product-compliance
Lightning Source LLC
Chambersburg PA
CBHW060851270326
41934CB00002B/99